THE DOMESTIC BLISS OF PLANTS

❖   EZEQUIEL N.   ❖

Translated by Arthur Malcolm Dixon
Foreword by Adalber Salas Hernández

𝒜
'Alliteratïon

THE DOMESTIC BLISS OF PLANTS | EZEQUIEL N.
Translated by Arthur Malcolm Dixon

First edition in English in September 2025

© Ezequiel N.
© Foreword by Adalber Salas Hernández
© Alliteratïon Publishing, 2025

www.thealliteration.us

Design by Elena Roosen
Cover by Andrea Martínez
Proofreading by Tess Rankin & Félix García
Editorial Coordination by Amayra Velón

ISBN: 979-8-9932429-1-0

A LOWERCASE POETICS: EZEQUIEL'S
THE DOMESTIC BLISS OF PLANTS

Intimacy is made of words. We all know it. Watershed words that separate inside from outside. Sometimes somewhat secret words, intimate names we have for our loved ones, our objects, our rituals. Other times, everyday words that get us through the daily grind and, having crossed the border of our inner life, start to look different, revealing nuances that only we can see.

The poetry of Ezequiel achieves an unusual feat: It shares with us this intimacy made of words. There are common, noisy, boastful feats in poetry. But there are also, on the rarest of occasions, quiet feats. The one Ezequiel's poetry achieves belongs to this discreet lineage. The texts that make up *The Domestic Bliss of Plants* trace the limits of a life lived without the uproar of the epic, a life of depth and details rich with meaning.

For example, the poem titled "After a long time walking" comes to mind:

After a long time walking

we reached the view
of a hidden lake.
We weren't planning
to stay there.
The sweet leaves

of the larches
over the frozen water.
A fox's mouth
was outlined in a cloud,
its teeth were so smooth.
You raised up your hand
with breadcrumbs
and the wind carried them away.

Ezequiel's poetry feeds on the contrast between outside and inside. This book boasts many landscapes, but their vastness is tamed by a human scale. Just like in "After a long time walking"—whose title, which is also its first line, highlights its lack of pretense—the view of the lake, the larches, and the clouds—elements that, in other hands, might reveal a pompous majesty or a sleep-deprived romanticism—surrender their magnitude to another scale, a miniscule one, of breadcrumbs on the palm of a hand. Suddenly, a vast expanse fits there, in that hand.

Likewise, a river can find itself contained in the image of a faucet with water running through it, as in the poem "An artificial river":

I gather water in my hands
to wash my face.
The faucet is an artificial river.
I turn it off and it is empty,
I turn it on and it refills.
I travel at my leisure down this river
that can no longer turn off.
The things that break
fill other things
until they overflow.
Is that poetry?

Doing something
that slips through your hands.

A river on a scale that is simply human. A current that, when interrupted, overflows and fills everyday life with its transparent, ductile poetry. Ezequiel is a sort of inverted landscapist: He brings the outside to the inside, transforming both into the same substance. The contrast is then resolved through a sort of spillage: Minimal human life, that sum of painful and pleasurable details, ends up pouring unpretentiously over the natural or urban landscape, over the everyday, instilling there its stunning smallness.

This lowercase poetics is so lacking in grandiloquence that we come across lines like these, from the poem "Refuge":

I went out to pee in the immensity
and felt like I was filling
all the frozen lakes of the south

The immensity is not devalued by this act—nor is it by the multitude of similar acts that fill *The Domestic Bliss of Plants*. Here, there is no ridicule. This is, instead, the integration of the landscape's elements into the intimacy of the self that unfurls throughout the book. They become natural elements of the self's own private realm. Acts such as these resolve the dichotomy between life within and space without, bringing everything toward the inside, making horizontal what we had learned to understand as exclusively vertical.

In this veiled fashion, Ezequiel's poetics are subversive: They take apart hierarchies of poetic discourse with the same simplicity with which they approach commonplace events. He builds an inhabitable intimacy in which we can recognize ourselves. An intimacy made of words that, in this book, he hands over to us.

Adalber Salas Hernández

THE DOMESTIC
BLISS OF PLANTS

El poema que me escribiría si fuera vos

Es la edad en que las chicas somos deformes.
Tenés un brazo más largo que el otro,
no aprendés a correr, te duelen
los pechos y no sabés bien
con qué cara mirar a Jesús.
Les conté a mis amigas
que en la cama
Ezequiel sólo me tocó la cara.
Fue como besar un fantasma. Ezequiel dijo
hablar con vos es ir
por un campo minado
y me hizo llorar.
Sentía que estaba bien llorar.
Me saqué fotos
y se las mandé a ellas.
Puede parecer que no sé estar triste
pero no es verdad.
La verdad es que no sé llorar por él y hay perros
que vi que lloran mejor que yo.
Paseamos todo el fin de semana,
nos dimos la mano cuando dijimos chau.
Él se quedó en la placita de los animales
apoyado en la réplica
de una jirafa. Me di la vuelta
para verlo: estiraba la mano
para saber qué tan alto era.
Bajito, sos bajito, no llegás a la mitad del cuello.

The poem I would write for me if I were you

At this age us girls are deformed.
One of your arms is longer than the other,
you don't get how to run, your breasts
hurt and you don't know which face
to wear to look at Jesus.
I told my friends
that in bed Ezequiel
just touched my face.
It was like kissing a ghost. Ezequiel said
talking to you is like
walking through a minefield
and it made me cry.
It felt okay to cry.
I took some photos of myself
and sent them to my friends.
It might seem like I don't know how to be sad
but that isn't true.
The truth is I don't know how to cry about him and
I've seen dogs cry better than me.
We walked around all weekend,
we shook hands when we said bye.
He stood there in the animal playground
leaning against the fake
giraffe. I turned around
to look at him: He held his hand up
high to see how tall he was.
Short, you're short, not even halfway up the neck.

Los tatuajes

Leí los poemas de mis amigos y sentí
que me contagiaban una tristeza idiota
de un modo superficial,
como esos tatuajes de figuritas de chicles
que se venden en las escuelas o esos tatuajes
de hena en la playa. Hena.
Eh no.
La respuesta de los adolescentes ante cualquier cosa
es primero negativa.
Desconfían de lo aparente,
no les hace gracia.

Tattoos

I read my friends' poems and felt
an idiotic sadness rub off on me,
superficially,
like those little tattoos on gum wrappers
they sell at school or those henna
tattoos they give you at the beach. Henna.
Heh, nah.
A teenager's response to anything,
at first, is negative.
They mistrust the apparent,
they don't get it.

Eno

Cuando me enteré que estabas embarazada
hice pis durante largos minutos, absorto,
miraba cómo el líquido llenaba
la taza del inodoro sin comprender
qué había dentro de mi cuerpo
o si era el flujo de tu sangre, tu ictericia,
que salía como un fantasma.

Me enteré que ibas a tener un hijo
mientras escuchaba una canción de Brian Eno.
Entonces comprendí lo que era una canción:
una sucesión de silencios atrapados
entre algunos ruidos. La vida también es eso,
pis que golpea contra un depósito
de agua estancada.

Tu cuerpo se encogía en la cama,
en una ciudad inundada,
cuando me enteré que ibas a tener un hijo.
Yo daba vueltas alrededor de tu casa.
Quería librarme de la maldición
de tomar diecisiete cervezas.
Entonces escuché que tu bebé lloraba
porque te habías dormido sobre su brazo
y no tenía las palabras
para pedirte que te hicieras a un lado.

Dejé la última lata sobre la ventana
y me fui a cambiar los muebles de lugar, flotaban.

Eno

When I found out you were pregnant
I pissed for several long minutes, engrossed,
watching how the liquid filled
the toilet bowl, not understanding
what was in my body
or if it was your blood flow, your jaundice
emerging like a ghost.

I found out you were going to have a child
while I was listening to a Brian Eno song.
That's when I understood what a song was:
a sequence of silences trapped
between some noises. Life is the same thing,
piss hitting a reservoir
of still water.

Your body was balling up in bed,
inside a flooded city,
when I found out you were going to have a child.
I walked laps around your house.
I wanted to free myself of the curse
of drinking seventeen beers.
Then I heard your baby crying
because you had fallen asleep on his arm
and he didn't have the words
to ask you to move over.

I left the last can on the windowsill
and went to move the furniture around. It floated.

Agua

El hombre que miro está nadando. Su cuerpo sumergido
hace estrellar las montañas. ¿Sabe que lo amo
y que visto este traje como de atardecer
para no saltar encima suyo?

El paisaje es una cosa informe
donde se superponen relieves como ojos, declives.
Nada amanece.

El hombre es verde; el paisaje azul. Mi sombra extraña
su mirada que explica los fenómenos de refracción.

El hombre nada.
El hombre que amo está nadando.
Él nada.
El nada.

Esta página es como la red de mis ojos.
Una lámina de agua nos separa.

Water

The man I'm looking at is swimming. His body, submerged,
makes mountains crack. Does he know I love him
and I put on this suit, like sunset,
so as not to jump all over him?

The landscape is a shapeless thing
where reliefs overlap like eyes, inclines.
In his wake. Nothing awakes.

The man is green, the landscape blue. My shadow misses
the look in his eyes that explains the phenomena of refraction.

The man swims. Man? Nothing.
The man I love is swimming.
Swimming.
Nothing.

This page is like the netting of my eyes.
A film of water keeping us apart.

Un río artificial

Junto agua entre las manos
para lavarme la cara.
La canilla es un río artificial.
La cierro y está vacía,
la abro y se vuelve a llenar.
Manejo este río a mi gusto
que ya no cierra más.
Las cosas que se rompen
llenan otras cosas
hasta desbordarlas.
¿Será eso la poesía?
Hacer algo
que se te va de las manos.

An artificial river

I gather water in my hands
to wash my face.
The faucet is an artificial river.
I turn it off and it is empty,
I turn it on and it refills.
I travel at my leisure down this river
that can no longer turn off.
The things that break
fill other things
until they overflow.
Is that poetry?
Doing something
that slips through your hands.

Todas las mañanas

David Hockney
dibuja flores en su i-pad
y se las envía a sus amigos
tallos
que no necesitan del sol
ni del agua

o por ahí sí

el sol
que lo despierta con un rayito
entre las persianas
de su departamento de Kensington High Street
rodeado de tiendas lujosas y cafecitos
y el agua fría de la canilla
con la que se lava las manos
y se refriega los ojos
frente al espejo

igual
que vos y yo

agua y sol
es todo lo que necesitamos
para crecer
y un poco de cuidado
que nos hablen cuando despertamos
que nos den la mano para cruzar la calle
que alguien nos diga

Every morning

David Hockney
draws flowers on his iPad
and sends them to his friends
stems
requiring neither sun
nor water

or maybe so

the sun
that wakes him with a little beam
between the blinds
of his Kensington High Street flat
surrounded by posh shops and cafés
and the cold tap water
with which he washes his hands
and rubs his eyes
in the mirror

just
like you and me

water and sun
are all we need
to grow
and some tending
being talked to upon waking
hands being held to cross the street
someone to tell us

en este lugar estás hermosa
sé que ayer fue un día feo pero hoy
en tu casilla de mail
tenés flores

dales de tu agua
alumbralas con tu sol
ellas van a cuidarte
te lo prometo

here you're beautiful
I know yesterday was a tough day but today
in your mailbox
you have flowers

give them some of your water
shine down on them with your sun
they're going to tend to you
I promise

into the wildness

volver en un colectivo
  oscuro
atravesando la montaña

  no perforarla sino
    bajar con la suavidad de un borracho
  o una canción de cuna

atravesar decía
la bruma
regresar
a mí mismo

    dentro del bondi unos muchachos
  espantan los restos del verano
      el miedo a caer por el barranco
con un poco de cumbia

la canción de cuna

cierro los ojos y estoy
en ningún lugar
de vuelta
parado frente al camping
un vaca me mira
y mastica
una bolsa de supermercado

    la cumbia se detiene
    cuando entramos a la ciudad

into the wildness

coming back in a dark
   bus
going through the mountain

   not piercing it but
      coming down as gentle as a drunk
 or lullaby

going through the fog
was saying
going back
to myself

      on the bus some guys
    shoo off the vestiges of summer
       the fear of falling off the cliff
with some cumbia

the lullaby

I close my eyes and I'm
nowhere
again
standing in front of the campsite
a cow stares at me
chewing
on a shopping bag

      the cumbia stops
      when we get to the city

sé
que el silencio va por dentro

en la estación
alguien me espera

                    I know
silence goes inside

        at the station
        somebody waits for me

Prepará la ensalada

con tres gotas de aceite
de oliva. Dejá que las hojas
se mezclen -ya sé, el otoño-,
y pisalas despacio, levantalas
en el aire, hacé
todo esto con cierta gracia
de chica de circo. Probala,
probá poner las estaciones
suspendidas
en un rizo de viento.
Algunas cosas solo
se mezclan con azar.

Get the salad ready

with three drops of olive
oil. Let the leaves
mix—I know, autumn—
and step on them slowly, lift them
in the air, do
all of this with some circus girl's
grace. Try it,
try placing the seasons
suspended
on a curl of wind.
Some things are only
mixed by chance.

Hace días murieron las plantas del balcón

miro lo que queda de ellas
un tallo largo y amarillo
inclinado
unas pocas hojas con manchitas blancas
y la tierra dura sobre la que parecen decir
no volverá a crecer la vida

es verdad que no me acordaba de ellas
y apenas si había escuchado mi propia voz
repitiendo los pasos de una receta aprendida
junto a la persiana abierta en otra estación

corro con un vaso lleno de agua
la luz del sol multiplica los contornos
en el vidrio
lo siento lo siento lo siento
el eco fantasma con el que me perdono

volverán las hojas verdes y robustas
el tallo tendrá la fuerza de un Aquiles
abriendo el pecho de Héctor con una lanza

esto es la vida
lo siento lo siento lo siento
gotas de rocío agua limpia

pongo las cosas en orden
dentro de mi cabeza cubro de tierra
las partes heridas como un animal que se lame
solo en el bosque
y espero que el silencio se llene de fantasías

The plants on the balcony died days ago

I look at what's left of them
a long yellow stalk
leaning
a few leaves with white blemishes
and the hard dirt from which they seem to say
life will not grow back

it's true, I had forgotten them
and barely heard my own voice
repeating steps to a recipe I'd learned
beside the open blinds in another season

I run with a glass full of water
the sunlight multiplies the outlines
on the glass
I'm sorry I'm sorry I'm sorry
the ghost echo with which I forgive myself

the plump green leaves will come back
the stalk will have the strength of an Achilles
opening Hector's chest with a spear

that's life
I'm sorry I'm sorry I'm sorry
dewdrops clean water

I put things in their place
in my head I cover up with earth
the wounded parts like an animal licking itself
alone in the forest
and I hope the silence will be filled with fantasies

brote a brote
le pido al sol
un poco de clemencia

bud to bud
I ask the sun
for just a little mercy

salir de los poemas de amor

como quien sale de una reunión sin que nadie se dé cuenta
los saludos en la mesa los billetes
restos de una cena en la que permaneceré callado
y luego ir
pero hacia dónde
los vestidos de las chicas que soñé
cuelgan cada día
en la soga de mi memoria
se secan al sol
se mojan cuando llueve
nadie viene a buscarlos

leaving love poems

like you leave a gathering without anyone noticing
the farewells at the table the banknotes
leftovers of a dinner at which I'll keep quiet
and then leave
but heading where
the dresses of the girls I dreamed about
hang every day
from the rope of my memory
drying in the sun
getting wet when it rains
nobody comes to get them

Miyó

En las mañanas heladas Miyó
atraviesa la playa con gaviotas,
la cajita de balas del mar.

Dispara contra la línea del horizonte
Miyó
en un all-inclusive del alma.

Encerrado, recoge piedras blancas, balas,
caracoles y cangrejos. Deja todo
junto a las gomas viejas y la carcasa
de una tv. Deja que la cosas
se habiten a sí mismas por un rato.
La palabra barranco, por ejemplo, se sienta
sobre el marco de la ventana y desde allí
mira llegar los camiones de mudanza.

Miyó escribe la palabra barranco.
Después se lava los pies en un charco de desagüe
y se pierde en la niebla y camina sobre la playa
y no le molestan las heladas.

Miyó

In the frosty mornings Miyó
walks across the beach with seagulls,
the sea's little box of shells.

He shoots at the horizon line
does Miyó
from an all-inclusive resort of the soul.

Locked in, he picks up white stones, bullets,
conches, crabs. He leaves everything
by the old tires and the carcass
of a TV set. He lets things
dwell inside themselves awhile.
The word *cliff*, for example, sits
upon the windowsill and from it
watches as the moving trucks arrive.

Miyó writes the word *cliff*.
Then he washes his feet in a puddle of drainpipe water
and is lost in mist and walks along the beach
and is unbothered by the frost.

Ducha

Partículas componen el paisaje: no hay cielo ni montañas,
solo unos azulejos marítimos, luces y sombras y rocío
sobre una planta de interior. La ropa amontonada antes del baño.
Un chico entre las cosas dobla su cuerpo
bajo el efecto multiforme de la canilla.

-el efecto la lluvia el chico
la ropa amontonada antes del baño-

Mientras el agua caiga sobre su espalda
un lento rumor robará mis ojos, un único pelo
en la bañera.
Su cuerpo cede. Alguien -no yo- alisa una toalla
con el método liviano de acariciar un animal dormido.

Es el nuevo rumor.

La canilla gira sobre su eje. La planta de interior respira
vapores sin brillo, partículas solamente.

Shower

Particles make up the landscape: There is neither sky nor
mountains,
just some seaside tiles, lights and shadows and dew
on a houseplant. The clothes piled up before the bath.
A boy among things bends his body
under the showerhead's multifarious influence.

—the influence the rain the boy
the clothes piled up before the bath—

While water falls against his back
a slow murmur will steal my eyes, a single hair
on the tub.
His body yields. Someone—not me—smooths out a towel
with the light method of stroking a sleeping animal.

This is the new murmur.

The faucet turns on its axis. The houseplant breathes in
unshining vapors, particles is all.

El jardín

Sí, voy a dar un paseo. Sí,
a caminar sobre esas flores.
Un animal que no tiene
un nombre hermoso
como Camila, Claudia o Dolores
mira el borrón de mi cara. Sí,
me detengo y quiero que me observen
ahora esos tipos que nunca van a abrir mi bata.
Un animal hermoso puede llamarse
y empujar como el viento. Nadie
me ha dicho el viento es tu canción y todavía
suena en ecos esos días que se alejan sobre el pasto.
Sí
voy a cantar esa canción
a cruzar por el jardín y saltar alambrados.

Mi yo suelta una pregunta como un diente de león
¿Te gustan las flores, los gusanos?

The garden

Yes, I'm going to take a walk. Yes,
to walk over these flowers.
An animal that does not have
a lovely name
like Camila, Claudia, or Dolores
looks at my smudge of a face. Yes,
I stop and I want them to look at me,
right now, these guys who'll never open up my robe.
A lovely animal can be named
and push like the wind. Nobody
has told me the wind is your song and still
rings in echoes these days that drift off over the grass.
Yes
I am going to sing this song
to cut across the garden and jump fences.

My self tosses out a question like a dandelion
Do you like flowers? And worms?

John

Está por llover
John lo sabe

Tiene puestos los anteojos de carey
que fueron míos
el tiempo en que fuimos centauros

Se desnuda en el balcón
la lluvia lo secuestrará

Pienso en su espalda atravesando
la ciudad de terrazas cables y jardines
el túnel callado en el que habito
tras los lentes oscuros

esos lentes que dejé sobre la mesa
junto a una nota que decía
volveré cuando la lluvia…

pero John
empapado y sediento
supo que mentí

John

It's about to rain
John knows it

He's wearing the tortoiseshell glasses
that were mine
when we were centaurs

He takes his clothes off on the balcony
the rain will take him away

I think of his back passing through
the city of terraces wires and gardens
the quiet tunnel where I dwell
behind dark lenses

those glasses I left on the table
next to a note that said
I'll be back when the rain...

but John
soaked through and thirsty
knew I was lying

Ustedes pueden terminar este poema por mí

En el pizarrón está escrito: Trabajar
cada día para que el ego
no aplaste su inteligencia.
Los estudiantes dibujan sobre las mesas.
Repito en silencio: trabajar cada día...
Cuando era chico caminaba
por una avenida congelada
de casa hacia la escuela
en una ciudad todavía oscura
a las 9am. Me acuerdo
de mis zapatos negros andando
como cucarachas por el asfalto
escarchado. Las manos se ponían
rojas por el frío y tenía
la sensación de poder ver el hueso
de mis nudillos traspasar la piel.
Ahora voy hacia el fondo
del salón, una luz amarilla y ruidos
de colectivos y peatones interrumpen
el desarrollo de la clase. No tengo
nada para enseñarles, creía
que podía llegar a ser un gran artista.
Trabajar cada día para que tu ego
no desprecie tu amor propio. Vamos,
el amor propio es diversión,
adelante, patinen en sus zapatos.
Vamos,
ustedes eligen a dónde
y pueden
resolverlo bien,
(son solo palabras).

You all can finish this poem for me

On the chalkboard is written: *Work*
every day so your ego
doesn't crush your intelligence.
The students draw on their desks.
I repeat, silently: Work every day…
When I was a kid I used to walk
down a frozen avenue
from home to school
in a city still dark
at 9 a.m. I remember
my black shoes stepping
like cockroaches across the frosty
asphalt. My hands would turn
red with cold and I felt
I could see the bones
of my knuckles show through my skin.
Now I walk to the back
of the classroom, a yellow light and noise
of buses and pedestrians disrupts
the class's progress. I have
nothing to teach them, I thought
I could become some great artist.
Work every day so your ego
won't look down on your self-love. Come on,
self-love is just for fun,
go on, skate in your shoes.
Come on,
you all pick where
and you can
work it out,
(they're only words).

Vamos,
ustedes pueden
terminar este
poema por mí.

Come on,
you all can
finish this
poem for me.

Después de caminar mucho tiempo

llegamos a la vista
de un lago escondido.
No pensábamos
quedarnos acá.
Las hojas dulces
de los alerces
sobre el agua helada.
Una boquita de zorro
se dibujó en una nube,
sus dientes eran tan suaves.
Vos alzaste tu mano
con migas de pan
y se las llevó el viento.

After a long time walking

we reached the view
of a hidden lake.
We weren't planning
to stay there.
The sweet leaves
of the larches
over the frozen water.
A fox's mouth
was outlined in a cloud,
its teeth were so smooth.
You raised up your hand
with breadcrumbs
and the wind carried them away.

Mis días felices

Con mi novia pintamos los muebles de la casa
de colores brillantes en la terraza del edificio
y después nos reímos de lo feo que quedan
y nos lamentamos y nos decimos
que nada es para siempre

Ya no quiero ser joven
ir a fiestas a arrancarme el corazón
con pasitos de baile secretos
con pasitos de baile prohibidos
para el cuerpo en el que habito.

Imagino entonces que soy una estrella melancólica
toda lunar enquistada en las puertas del cielo
y pido un deseo para mi yo de abajo

    que Ezequiel pueda vestirse de mujer sin tener vergüenza
    que se pinte los labios con aerosoles
    y el alma con brillantina
    que su barba crezca como un río
    y que sus palabras se queden con el viento
    que el peronismo gane las elecciones
    que el pasto sea no-binario, es irónico,
    que sea pasto y nada más
    que los recibos de sueldos vengan con flores
    y que los jubilados vivan como reyes

Ya no deseo nada para mí
Me divierto pensando que una vez estuve triste
y que una poeta me dijo Sos un hombre de cristal
Sí

My happy days

My girlfriend and I painted the furniture
vivid colors on the building's terrace
then we laughed at how ugly it looked
and we regretted it and told each other
nothing lasts forever.

I don't want to be young anymore
go rip my heart out at parties
with dance moves secret
with dance moves forbidden
to the body I inhabit.

So I imagine I'm a melancholy star
every beauty mark embedded in the heavens' doors
and I ask for one wish for my self who's down here

    may Ezequiel dress as a woman and not feel ashamed
    may he spray-paint his lips
    and slick down his soul
    may his beard grow like a river
    and his words go with the wind
    may the Peronists win the elections
    may the grass be nonbinary, it's ironic,
    may the grass be grass and nothing more
    may the payslips come with flowers
    and the retired live like royalty

I wish for nothing for myself
I am amused to think I once was sad
and a poet, a woman, told me You're a glass man
Yes

Soy un hombre de cristal
y me rompí
Nunca quise ser una dama de hierro

Aspiro las esquirlas
le doy de comer a las gatas
pongo en orden la cama y la casa
prendo una velita y bailo dócilmente
la alegría doméstica de las plantas

Estoy contento de haber llegado hasta acá
Ya no soy joven, pero somos hermosos.

I am a glass man
and I broke myself
I never wished to be an iron lady

I vacuum up the shards
I feed the cats
I tidy up the bed, the house
I light a candle and I meekly dance
to the domestic bliss of plants

I'm happy to have made it here
I am no longer young, but we are beautiful.

Koan zen

Una vez me trepé a los techos y nadie corrió en mi ayuda.
No existe una forma de irse sin dejar huella.
Quiero correr pero me agito.
Nadie dice cuando algo es un buen poema
pero sí es posible escuchar
seguí intentando.
No podés saber cuándo vas a dar el salto
aunque pases toda tu vida parado sobre el borde
o hayas tomado carrera como una honda que se estira
y cuando finalmente decidas que llegó el momento,
que estás cansado de tanto ir para atrás
y que ya nada puede detenerte
porque naciste para eso, entonces
es mejor que esperés un poco más
(nadie puede decirte cuánto tiempo)
porque quizás no estés saltando desde el techo de tu casa
hacia algo grande como un abismo,
por ahí solamente estás despierto una mañana
pensando que ese día va a ser distinto
y alguien va a decirte no lo hagás,
te vas a romper la cabeza.
Pero vos ya esperaste lo suficiente,
respiraste más de un minuto bajo el agua
casi dos
y te das cuenta de que no se trata de saltar
ni siquiera de ir hacia adelante o hacia arriba,
que todo este tiempo estuviste aguantando.
No vas a matar a alguien porque vos no harías eso
sino lo que dice el koan zen
que por ser oriental y no tener un origen claro

Zen koan

Once I climbed up on the rooftop and no one came running to
my aid.
There is no way to leave without leaving a trace.
I want to run but I get nervous.
No one says when it's a good poem
but you can hear it
I kept on trying.
You can't know when you're going to jump
even if you spend your whole life standing on the edge
or you have gained momentum like a tensing sling
and when you finally decide the moment's come
you're tired of so many steps backward
and nothing can stop you anymore
for you were born for this, so
it is best you wait a little longer
(nobody can tell you how much time)
because maybe you're not jumping off the roof of your house
into something as big as an abyss,
perhaps you're just awake one morning
thinking today will be different
and somebody will tell you not to do it,
you're going to bust your head open.
But you have waited long enough,
you breathed over a minute underwater
almost two
and you realize it's not about jumping
or even going forward or upward,
and you were dealing with it this whole time.
You're not about to kill somebody because you wouldn't do that
but, instead, you follow the Zen koan,
which being Far Eastern and lacking a clear origin

como la comida que saboreás cada noche
te inspira confianza.

Cavá tan profundo como puedas
hasta que el pozo se convierta en montaña.

just like the food you savor every night
you find trustworthy.

Dig as deep as you can
till the well becomes a mountain.

Refugio

llegamos al refugio en la montaña
cuando los pies todavía vibraban
descalzos en la quietud
donde nos hundimos

ya se nos hace la noche
dijiste blandamente
pero parecía que la noche
nos hacía a nosotros

salí a orinar en la inmensidad
y sentí que llenaba
todos los lagos helados del sur

llené mi corazón
con las piedras
llevé en las piedras
las heladas
regué mi corazón con el agua
de todos los lagos helados del sur

al dormirte dijiste una palabra
suave campante acompasada
amanecía
en esa ladera querida de Dios

Refuge

we made it to the mountain refuge
with our feet still shivering
shoes off in the stillness
where we sank

night is falling on us
you said softly
but it seemed like night
was falling in us

I went out to pee in the immensity
and felt like I was filling
all the frozen lakes of the south

I filled my heart
with stones
I carried in the stones
the frosts
I irrigated my heart with the water
of all the frozen lakes of the south

when you went to sleep you said a word
smooth measured nonchalant
the dawn was breaking
on this mountainside beloved by God

Distorsión

El contorno de una montaña sobre el ala del avión.
Al otro lado del teléfono, sonidos insignificantes
como sacar una foto dentro de un sueño.
Tu voz arrastra una mala compañía.
A esto también le llaman amor.
No quiero despertar en el sentido
de saber que estamos en el aire,
más allá de cualquier accidente geográfico.
Tuve que encerrar mi capacidad de decir lo que me altera.
Ahora el camino parece una tarde en un bosque nevado.
El auto blanco de frío a un costado de la ruta.
Algunos asientos más adelante
me pregunto si todavía sentís miedo,
envuelta en auriculares, sin gestos
que permitan identificar lo que te pasa.
Dentro de dos horas voy a llegar hasta vos
pero no voy a poder verte, como un chico
que se queda dormido
en la mejor parte del viaje.
Ahora caliento agua para té
y olvido lo que conversamos.

El paraíso está lejos del ala congelada.
Nos piden calma para situaciones que nunca antes vivimos.
Que permanezcamos sentados en los asientos.
Somos incapaces de otra cosa. Miré tus ojos
tan de cerca
que parecían animales cansados bajo una lluvia fría.
La paciencia de no poder hacer más que esto:
sostengo tu cabeza   mientras dentro tuyo
pasa algo que nunca va a alcanzarme.
Te pronunciás contra toda distorsión.

Distortion

The outline of a mountain on the plane's wing.
Down the phone line, sounds insignificant
as taking a photo in a dream.
Your voice drags bad company behind it.
That's also something they call love.
I don't want to wake up in the sense
of knowing we are in the air,
beyond any geographic accident.
I had to lock away my knack for saying what upsets me.
Now the path looks like an evening in a snowy forest.
The car white with cold to one side of the road.
Some seats ahead
I wonder if you're still afraid,
wrapped up in headphones, no expression
to discern what's going on with you.
I'll get to you within two hours
but can't see you, like a kid
who falls asleep
at the best part of the trip.
Now I put the kettle on for tea
and forget what we were talking about.

> Heaven is far from the frozen wing.
> They tell us to stay calm in situations we've never
> been through before.
> To remain in our seats.
> We can do nothing else. I looked into your eyes
> so close
> they looked like tired animals under cold rain.
> The patience of being unable to do more than this:
> I hold your head   while inside you
> something is happening that will never reach me.

Cuando tenía 7 meses
los médicos sacaron uno de mis ojos
para operarme de estrabismo
y perdí el sentido de la distancia.

You state your opposition to any and all distortion.
When I was seven months old
the doctors took out one of my eyes
to correct my strabismus
and I lost my sense of distance.

Estrellas en el fondo del río

Ese día subimos a la pirámide
porque el guía nos dijo que desde ahí
podía verse el atardecer
-el más feliz ocaso de sus vidas-
cuando llegamos arriba había una mujer
montando su negocio   dibujaba
el horizonte en unas hojas amarillas muy gastadas
y las tiraba una a una a medida que terminaba
con tantas ganas que no miraba a nadie
y todos la veíamos a ella
pronto el sol dejó de caer y cayó la noche
la mujer se dio vuelta y frente a nosotros
estiró su pollera oscura con dobladillos
y algunos entendieron y otros se sintieron estafados y otros
más tontos tal vez como nosotros
nos quedamos mirando cómo
caían monedas sobre su pollera
que poco a poco se iluminaba
estrellas en el fondo del río

Stars on the riverbed

That day we climbed the pyramid
because the guide told us from up there
you could see the sunset
—the happiest twilight of your lives—
when we got up there we found a woman
setting up shop   drawing
the horizon on some worn-out yellow pages
and pulling them out one at a time as she finished
so focused she was not looking at anyone
and all of us were watching her
the sun suddenly ceased to set and night fell
the woman turned and out to us
she stretched her dark hemmed skirt
some understood and others felt swindled and others
stupider, perhaps, like us
just stood there watching how
coins came falling into her skirt
which bit by bit lit up
stars on the riverbed

Sueño que Allen Ginsberg me da la mano y cruzamos el mar

Navegábamos
en balsas
de bambú.
Nos decíamos
poemas
de balsa
a balsa.
Una conversación
sin interrupciones.
Tu pelo
lleno
de algas
marinas.
Tu barba
o la de un
pirata
melancólico.
Cuando me desperté
me había
hecho pis
y estaba
desnudo.
Así debe oler
el paraíso,
me dije
Olor
a cholga
decía mamá.

I dream Allen Ginsberg takes my hand and we cross the sea

We were sailing
on bamboo
rafts.
We were reciting
poems
to each other, raft
to raft.
A conversation lacking
interruptions.
Your hair
full
of sea
weed.
Your beard
or a
melancholy
pirate's.
When I woke up
I had
pissed
and I was
naked.
This is what heaven
must smell like
I said to myself
Smells like
mussels
mom would say.

Cándido

Sobre la cabeza de un caballo muerto
hay un fueguito que parece una estrella,
al paso al trote al paso.
Alguien dice
estas son cosas que nunca antes escribiste.
Yo estoy vacío, vacío
al paso voy al trote al paso.
El corazón del caballo no es un faro
pero me guía en este páramo.
Cuando me vaya galopando, ¿habrá una estrella para mí?
Y si esa estrella no está o está enferma o ya murió,
¿eso quiere decir que no va a haber un fuego para mí?
Mi cabeza no tiene antenas. No capto las señales
y estoy obligado a hacer un trabajo
que no quiero,
el amor ya no me parece posible.

¡Corramos ahora que podemos!
¡Levantemos las espadas para cortar el cielo!
No importa si una nube de pólvora nos vuela la mano.
Al paso al trote al paso. Las espadas en el aire,
las patas de mi caballo galopan este desierto
y voy a buscarte.

Naive

Over the head of a dead horse
there hangs a little fire like a star,
walking trotting walking.
Someone says
you never wrote these things before.
I'm empty, empty
walking I am trotting walking.
The horse's heart is not a lighthouse
but it guides me through this barren land.
When I start galloping, will there be a star for me?
And if that star is absent or is ill or dead,
does that mean there will be no fire for me?
My head has no antennae. I don't catch the signals
and I'm forced to do a job
I do not want,
I no longer think love is possible.

Let's run now while we can!
Let's raise our swords to cut the sky!
It doesn't matter if a cloud of powder blows our hand away.
Walking trotting walking. Swords in the air,
my horse's hooves gallop over this desert
and I'm coming for you.

Un campo de flores

Me tatué para ir a verte
jugar con ese chico que no es tu hermano
sobre la misma cama donde antes,
mucho antes, habías dibujado un campo
de flores en mi espalda.

Ahora es tu espalda la que veo
desde otra habitación bajo unas alas enormes
que sacuden el polvo de la que era nuestra biblioteca.

Es inútil comprar una almohada nueva,
dar vuelta el colchón, esconder los discos
que escuchábamos por esos días
en que dibujabas campos de flores y firmabas
con tu nombre sobre mi cuerpo.

Me tatué para ir a verte.
Un campo de flores en mi espalda.

A field of flowers

I got a tattoo to come see you
to play with that kid who's not your brother
on the same bed where before,
a long time before, you drew a field
of flowers on my back.

Now it's your back I see
from another room under enormous wings
that shake the dust off what was once our library.

It's useless buying a new pillow,
flipping the mattress, hiding the albums
we used to listen to back then
when you would draw fields of flowers and sign
your name on my body.

I got a tattoo to come see you.
A field of flowers on my back.

Ahora mi alma canta en un pájaro terrible de esta ciudad

a las cuatro de la mañana los balcones están cerrados
dentro de los departamentos hay chicos y chicas que lloran
uñas largas y cuidadas

he vuelto a escribir poesía pero sigo lejos de mi corazón
escucho su ruidito y sospecho que chispea en algún lugar
te pido que me lleves hasta ahí que no dejes
que vaya solo

las calles se enredan
y tengo un caleidoscopio dentro del pecho

esta es la única manera que conozco de estar triste
una línea larga junto a otra que no la cruza nunca
pero está llena de nudos

tu barrio queda mucho más lejos
y tu casa perdida dentro de mis ojos
todo me lo trago y al mismo tiempo no trago nada
como un agujero negro

cuando termine la noche
cuando el sol aparezca tonto e incansable
voy a estar a mitad de camino
en medio de esta selva oscura
y tal vez por casualidad nos crucemos
y me digas acá está lo que andabas buscando

el corazón es un cazador solitario

Now my soul sings in a terrible bird of this city

at four in the morning the balcony doors are shut
in the apartments are boys and girls crying
long well-tended nails

I am writing poetry again but still far from my heart
I hear its little noise and suspect somewhere it is giving off

                                                                     sparks

I ask you to take me there to not let
me go alone

the streets get tangled
and I have a kaleidoscope in my chest

this is the only way I know to be sad
a long line alongside another that never crosses it
but is full of knots

your neighborhood is much further away
and your house lost in my eyes
I swallow everything and at the same time swallow nothing
like a black hole

when the night ends
when the sun appears silly and tireless
I'll be halfway there
in the middle of this dark jungle
and maybe by chance we will cross paths
and you will tell me *here's what you were looking for*

the heart is a lonely hunter

INDEX

A

THE DOMESTIC BLISS OF PLANTS | EZEQUIEL N.

Made in Miami Beach ~ Printing as needed

◊◊◊

2025

www.ingramcontent.com/pod-product-compliance
Lightning Source LLC
Chambersburg PA
CBHW020216090426